11/2000

Armen -

I think of you already

dancing

Things to do

pictures and verse
by
Sandra Magsamen

Life is not as complicated as some may say...
here are a few simple things to do to guide you along the way.

Things to do
count your blessings
aim high
laugh out loud

Embrace
the world
with your own
genuine
style...

and think
with your heart
instead
of your head
for
awhile.

Strive
to grow and
challenge
yourself
each day...

and count
the
blessings
that come
your way.

Don't listen to people who say no...

follow your dreams with passion wherever they go.

Some days
will bring
problems
and
turn your
smile upside
down...

be flexible
when finding
solutions;
the best
answers are
often creatively
found.

Believe
in something
worthwhile
and with
vision
see it through...

and give other people credit where credit is due.

thank you

Make time to laugh with family and friend's, and celebrate each other and the support every person lends.

Life
is a journey
that
twists
and turns...

a
winding road
of experiences
offering
much to
learn.

Use
Your heart as a
compass and set
out on your way—
there's no better
time to start
than today.

Pictures and verse by Sandra Magsamen

Exclusive licensing agent Momentum Partners, Inc., NY, NY

S Editions is an imprint of SMITHMARK Publishers.

This edition published in 1999 by SMITHMARK Publishers, a division of U.S. Media Holdings, Inc., 115 West 18th Street, New York, NY 10011

S Editions book are available for bulk purchase for sales promotion and premium use. For details write or call the manager of special sales, S Editions, 115 West 18th Street, New York, NY 10011; 212-519-1215.

Distributed in the U.S. by Stewart, Tabori & Chang, a division of U.S. Media Holdings, Inc., 115 West 18th Street, New York, NY 10011.

ISBN: 1-55670-897-1
Printed in Hong Kong

1 0 9 8 7 6 5 4 3 2 1